MW01247962

Standing Naked in the Rain

Standing Naked in the Rain

A Story about a *Good* Dog

BRET NICKS

Charleston, SC
www.PalmettoPublishing.com

Standing Naked in the Rain
Copyright © 2021 by Bret Nicks

First Edition

Hardcover ISBN: 978-1-68515-292-5
Paperback ISBN: 978-1-68515-293-2
eBook ISBN: 978-1-68515-294-9

To Mandy, Mikayla, Blake,
and dog lovers everywhere—
cherish the memories!

Contents

CHAPTER 1:

The Selection

HAVE YOU EVER WALKED INTO A HUMANE SOCIETY or animal shelter? The sights and the sounds are memorable for most, creating a lifelong neurosynaptic imprint. There, in restricted quarters, are myriad animals—dogs and cats of various ages, breeds, colors, and personalities. A virtual potpourri of potential pets yearning for an opportunity to find a family—and those looking for a new pet, feeling much the same.

For me the thought of a new puppy conjured mental images of unbridled joy wrapped in a warm, wriggling bundle of unconditional love. The anticipation of what might be mixed with the sounds of barking—seasoned and youthful—brought me back to the days of my youth, when experiencing something for the first time would overwhelm my spirit. At first, walking into the adoption area, I was acutely aware of the care taken and cleanliness ensured by the incredible team of volunteers. The smell of animals was present but balanced with a gentle cleanliness that set my olfactory senses to rest.

At first there was only an intermittent bark, followed by a few welcoming meows coming from the cat cages lining the facility entrance. Some eagerly moved forward and rubbed along the facing of the cage, hoping for a gentle touch. Others would remain in the back of their domicile, afraid to embrace the possibility of something greater, something better than what they had known so far. Their eyes pensive but penetrating—looking for hope, hoping for love. As a lover of all animals, I smiled with my face—and my eyes—as my heart broke for each one, knowing that I was not there that day to find a feline friend.

However, in the moments to follow, I found myself standing amid a virtual canine heaven. A plethora of wriggling puppies climbing all over each other, young dogs pausing in momentary attention to those who had just arrived, and those with more mature dispositions all anxiously awaited the same outcome—someone to take them home. All colors and sizes of mixed breeds were present. But I was drawn to the large, caged area toward the back. There, nine puppies were jumping and rolling about like an infantile, playful mosh pit at an early Lollapalooza concert, only with the sounds of puppy play instead of deafening grunge music.

The more docile puppies were gathered toward the middle and had become the targets of the others. Chewing on ears, nibbling on tiny paws, toppling over each other in a wriggling mass of pure bliss. And that energy, it was contagious. Not that I felt like chewing on ears or trying to reach, let alone nibble on my toes—but the air was full of excitement. Unknowingly, one of these little bundles of joy would soon change our world.

I like candy. And walking into an old-school candy shop, like the Mast General Stores of the world, sets me off. So many choices. Each candy with its own unique flavor and characteristics—and many chock-full of confectionary-associated memories from the past. That moment in the humane society was no different.

In that large cage, there were nine puppies. Black, brown, and those just like any box of chocolate mixed just right. Some trying to sleep, others nibbling on the ears of those trying to rest. Tails wagging incessantly and bodies tumbling over each other in barrel rolls of energy. Each with their own unique characteristics, and—just like that kid in the candy store—I felt excited uncertainty about which to choose. Although amid the activity of this wriggling mass of puppy play, there was one that stood out. Perhaps it was the way he seemed to be bounding into the endless mix of this canine cage match or how he would chase his tail relentlessly, only to find it remained just out of reach. Maybe it was how, after attacking his siblings, he would run over toward us looking like a masked marauder seeking applause or at least acknowledgement for this covert puppy approach.

Sometimes you just know. And with Toby (the name he would soon adopt), it was just like that.

CHAPTER 2:

Standing Naked in the Rain

PUPPY MADNESS. YES, IT IS A DIAGNOSABLE CONDItion. I've had it. So has my wife. Apparently, it only gets worse with age, and the level of amnesia it causes is evidently far worse than that of having a newborn child. Fooled by the soft coat, those deep puppy eyes, endless cuddles, and the delectable eau de toilette affectionately known as puppy breath, most owners lay to waste memories of the impending weeks if not months of nightly potty rounds. If anyone would have tried to remind me of this domestic routine, I would most certainly have downplayed the entire conversation. After all, it can't be that bad, right?

Inevitably, just when you are dropping into that elusively restorative deep sleep or at the climax of your Nicholas-Sparks-equivalent heartbreak dream, you hear it—the whimper. Not just once. *Whimper.* But repeatedly. *Whimper.* Growing in intensity like that gnawing of your stomach long before your next meal during a fast—or that dream that replays the same scene repeatedly. *Whimper.* That unrelenting whimpering triggered by a bladder under pressure—and a puppy that wants to relieve it. *Whimper.* Rather than face the consequences of a floor-bound pee fest, I had to overcome the incredible pull of gravity magnified by the forthcoming loss of comforting warmth and begrudgingly sit up. *Whimper.* With eyelids held fast by invisible weights, I attempted to force visual clarity despite the present darkness.

As I woke from sleep and stumbled from bed, disillusioned by the feigning rest opportunity given up, not quite certain why I emerged from the warmth of grandma's feather bed, I was lulled to the crate of the canine like a sailor to the song of a siren. Yet in the darkness of night, this was no small task.

Finding Toby amid the darkness was more like playing Marco Polo with a lovable creature that was neither historic nor an explorer—and, fortunately, whose only retort failed to move. Of course, feigning alertness didn't help with the realization that Toby was in the same place he was when the first REM cycle was sought—his crate.

The greater challenge came while fumbling with the door to the puppy crate—like picking a lock without clear sight and with hands and eyes that could barely coordinate the simplest of actions. Sleep deprivation will do that to you. Just ask a parent of a newborn child—or one with a new puppy. After fumbling with several attempts, looking more like an episode of Harold Lloyd trying to enter a revolving door or the Keystone Cops opening a prison cell, success would be mine.

Despite fumbling to find his collar and leash while volleying the endless nighttime licks and kisses and Toby frantically wriggling with the joy of impending freedom, we were ready to release

9

the grip of the bladder fairy. Barely awake, I shuffled toward the door, stumbling over an overturned umbrella as we exited the house. It is one thing to walk outside in the dark of the night when the weather is pleasantly warm and inviting. It is quite another when, halfway outside, you realize Mother Nature had released the horizontal rain weather-banshees that did little more than laugh at my attire, let alone my attempt to keep dry under cover of an umbrella. It wasn't a bomb cyclone, but certainly felt like it through the fog in my mind.

The tree branches waved; the trunks bent under the incessant wind. Large raindrops fell from the branches, adding a vertical attack to the raindrops falling from the clouds and saturating everything from my shoulders down. With the hope of not being seen by anyone at this time of night, we moved quickly to the place— that dedicated location in the yard where business was conducted, and no one asked questions.

As we slogged up the rain-saturated hill in the back-yard, I could barely see my footing on the spongelike terrain. Saturated and dripping wet, Toby led the climb to the top. Standing there in the wind, he didn't take the usual position of relief, but rather leaned into the wind. Snout forward, head lifted, and chest out—as if pointing toward a deer upwind of where we were standing. For what seemed like an eternity, he stood motionless and silent aside from the intermittent flaring of his nostrils. Even as I felt my body enact my autonomic responses to fight off early hypothermia in this cold, persistent wind, torrential rain, and less-than-ideal clothing, no verbal encouragement from me to finish his business led to any notable change in Toby's posture.

Behind us, car lights from the road twenty feet below passing intermittently created a silhouette that certainly could have set into motion even the most subdued of imaginations. Here amid the blustery night, standing on a hill, were a man and his dog in the rain. Unfortunately, the body-clinging, rain-soaked nighttime attire presented quite a silhouette for those passing in the night. No wonder there were murmurs in the coming weeks of a man and his dog standing naked in the rain.

Over the next months, the frequency of our clandestine midnight activities would wane. Falling into deep sleep would once again progress into a night of restoration, of revitalization. And for Toby, night would no longer hold the same mystique. The hillside midnight escape was replaced with a warm bed and recurrent dreams of suckling alongside his littermates when he was a newborn puppy. Eventually that dream was replaced by the most recent adventure with his family. Predictable? Certainly. Boring? Not at all.

CHAPTER 3:

Fear the Rabid Squirrel

AUTUMN IN NORTH CAROLINA IS PERHAPS MY FA-vorite season. The warmth of the waning summer sun has released its incessant grip on humidity. The vibrant sunrises and refreshing morning air deeply refuel the soul while concurrently transforming the leaves and landscape. If you've never seen the Blue Ridge this time of year, add it to your bucket list.

It is also a time when the squirrels begin their routine collections for the coming winter. As one might expect, any curious puppy would find these small creatures with broad, furry tails jumping and collecting about the yard something of interest. Especially a puppy of a sporting genetic code and an inquisitive spirit. Of course, what could possibly go wrong with a yard full of fastidious squirrels and the early attempts at canine underground electric fence training? What could indeed? I'll leave that for you to ponder.

After taking his quintessential position at the top of the front yard, the perfect vantage point for any ongoing neighborhood activities, Toby strolled around into the driveway like an undersized, undertrained watchdog making his rounds. It was at that point that he saw it. Moving intermittently. A svelte gray body articulated by a flowing plume of a tail that punctuated and balanced the body's intermittent motions. Stopping, it looked about and then continued its deliberate path to whatever seemed to have fallen nearby.

With ears raised in curiosity, Toby pensively moved up the driveway toward the edge of the yard. With each step forward, the squirrel became increasingly aware of the imposing spectator. Several hops, mirrored by several approaching steps. And with each step, Toby's eyes laser focused on this odd little creature precariously venturing along the edge of the yard.

And then it happened. With a burst of speed, the squirrel darted up the grassy ridge to the edge of the yard and bounded up and around to the hillside. And without hesitation, so did Toby. The squirrel scampered onto the canopied shelter that the hillside provided, while Toby, without considering for a moment the

ensuing impact of the electric, invisible wall—fortunately not quite 121 gigawatts of power.

I've often heard that ignorance is bliss. I suspect the one who coined that phrase was not wearing a shock collar around their neck. Unfortunately, I cannot say the same for myself—due to a personal electric collar misadventure, but that's an entirely different story.

As any overwhelmingly excited puppy engaged in the chase of a new, fuzzy moving object would respond, Toby ignored the three-second warning chirps of the impending effects of Ben Franklin's experiment from centuries gone by. The squirrel zigged; Toby zagged. And at the same moment that the squirrel launched into the bushes in a Cirque-du-Squirrel-eil fashion only inches away from the canine's snout, an electrical eruption triggered a fierce spasm about Toby's neck. Whether the realization of the collar-based electrical impact on his nuchal musculature or the thought that that fearless, perhaps rabid squirrel had ricocheted out of the bushes and begun attacking his neck crossed his mind, the effect was the same: a series of piercing yelps followed by a dog moving at breakneck speed across the variable landscape of the backyard. Never had Toby moved more swiftly, likely breaking a land-speed record without seemingly having a single paw touch the ground. Our bent-necked pooch reaching superhero status…at least for the moment.

By the time the series of shocks ceased, Toby had blazed across the yard, launched over the retaining

wall, and was sitting at the back door. For a moment it appeared that perhaps the collar setting may have been a little too robust, as there was steam rising from around Toby. On second glance there was no cause for concern about collar-associated thermal injury. Rather, the steam was rising from a rapidly expanding pool of darkness along the cold deck boards underfoot. Toby looked back, sheepishly sitting in a rapidly expanding pool of urine—an involuntary response to the perceived squirrel attack and the autonomic response that followed.

From that day forward, a peaceful truce had been declared in Toby's mind. The squirrels that ventured into our yard could gather the annual windfall of acorns, foraging without interruption or fear that Toby would even look twice in their direction. On occasion we would see him exploring the yard while the squirrels scurried about. And at times we thought we could still see a muscle memory response triggering a subtle nuchal spasm. Or perhaps it was just Toby shaking his head to alert the squirrels that he would no longer let his curiosity be seen as an impending attack.

CHAPTER 4:

Daily Manna

I GREW UP HEARING THE PHRASE "DON'T LOOK A GIFT horse in the mouth"—simply stated, when receiving a gift, be grateful for what it is, and don't imply you wished for something better. Attributed to John Heywood, this first appeared in English print in 1546. But for Toby this proverbial insight was as pertinent as ever. After all, for a dog motivated by food, is it not impossible to pass up a tasty morsel from heaven? Well, that was how Toby saw it.

Routine. Each of us have it to some degree. After the beginning of the day, you find yourself engrossed at work or working at home. Hours pass as you are laboring away when that time comes. Perhaps it is a set time or a unique sound that triggers the moment you crave a tiny morsel of goodness. I had a job once where every morning at nine forty-five, the morning snack truck would pull up, toot its recognizable horn, and like clockwork, all those working in the shop would hustle outside. With steam rising from the side of the truck, the incredible smells of warm pastries, breakfast sandwiches, donuts, and hot beverages filled the senses. What a splendid routine.

What is it for you? Perhaps it's a recognizable sound or just knowing it's that time of day for some gastrological indulgence that triggers your mouth to start salivating and your hunger pains to elicit your natural response toward food. For Toby it was the near daily service that despite rain, snow, sleet, or sunshine would provide such a momentary delicacy that it had become a hardwired response, better than Pavlov's training itself. Yes, still to this day, the USPS delivers.

From the early puppy days forward, Alan, our local USPS delivery specialist, took an interest in Toby. And the interest was mutual. It started with the simple greeting of our young puppy as he placed the mail in our box or occasionally walked up the sidewalk to drop a package at the door. Toby would wage his tail, flare his nostrils, and inhale in a manner that seemed to overwhelm his olfactory senses with the millions of scents he was able to capture.

In time, those verbal greetings progressed to the introduction of a little crunchy biscuit. With the quick flip of his wrist, Alan brought endless glee for a puppy heavily motivated by food. That first exchange was then followed by subsequent days where Alan would rumble down

Burbank Lane, tossing yet another delectable morsel into the driveway as he made his mail-drop approach. With the precision of an artillery specialist, he would land the surprise gift far enough inside the invisible fence that the rabid squirrel would not attack again but close enough that Toby would soon recognize the deliverer of this daily manna.

As this routine developed, so did the predictable response of a gastronomically motivated dog, especially when it came to biscuits from heaven. Internal clock? Check. Weather? Not a concern. Secondary sounds of intermittent squeaky brakes approaching from a distance? Check. Repetitive clicking sound from mailboxes being closed? Check. The bubbly retort of muffler sounds taken straight out of Willy Wonka's chocolate factory? Check. And with each of these recognizable triggers, the incessant excitement within Toby would no longer be contained. With wild abandon he would ring the bell at the back door (yes, he was trained to ring the bell to go outside). If that didn't garner the anticipated response, he would bolt to the front door and bark until freedom was his.

On those days when he was home alone, one can only imagine the anticipation turned to sorrow as he saw the gift truck come and go as the mail was being delivered. While ringing the bell and barking at the door would provide no response, Toby soon came to realize that quite often, the gift was still delivered even in his visual absence. He was not forgotten. And quite honestly, we are certain that all the neighbors knew when it was mail time simply by the barking fervor elicited by Toby.

While the gift received was not substantial, it was a gift, nonetheless. Something given freely, something given without expectation of anything in return, something given just because. Something like the relationship between a dog and its owner.

For Toby it created a daily moment that brought incredible anticipation and unfettered excitement. Perhaps there is a simple lesson in this for each of us. What is it that we do every day that brings great anticipation and unparalleled joy to those whose lives we touch? Perhaps it's our time to bring a little manna from heaven. Alan did just that. And Toby thought it was a great idea.

CHAPTER 5:

Sink or Swim

FOR THOSE WHO LIKE TO KEEP THINGS SIMPLE, ES-pecially the key attributes of your dog's breed, I have always placed the word "Labrador" and "swimming" in proximity. Every sporting dog owner has it. That dream of their canine launching into a body of water that is smooth as glass while jumping for that enviable, buoyant object of desire and creating a rippling effect that is only disrupted by the ensuing dog paddle. Like any parent of a baby just learning to walk, the hopeful images fantastically created of Toby in slow motion played over and over in my mind. The approach, full stride, the leap, the grasp, the entry, and the triumphant paddle. Toby could be the Carl Lewis of canines! Simply glorious.

Yes, we had visions of grandeur for Toby. Although apparently we failed in our parental duties to inform Toby of our expectations. His mother was a Lab—so why would he not have that innate swimming gene that was immediately triggered at the sight of any body of water greater than the puddle in the street? What possible breach of Labrador training etiquette could hinder what we perceived to be the next four-pawed hybrid of Michael Phelps and Carl Lewis in a canine coat?

The day of his aquatic coming-of-age had come. Wrapped in the glorious warmth and colors of autumn along the Blue Ridge Parkway, we set out. The air was crisp and sweet, like the first bite of a freshly picked Pink Lady. The water was calm and reflected the incredible views in all directions. As we approached the water, our anticipation was likely only matched by the inquisitive nature of a puppy seeing this all for the first time.

Kayak into the water. Paddles in hand. And Toby precariously placed between the fore and aft cockpits. It was glorious. The sun-soaked trees glistened in the early midday sun with myriad colors celebrating the end of summer and the ensuing winter. The Blue Ridge Mountains creating the most picturesque backdrop about the lake. And the whimpering of Toby as he pawed about the limited space surrounded by the sparkling abyss.

Toby was never one to miss out on the opportunity to "go for a ride." That typically meant jumping into the back seat of the truck, finding his blanket, and hoping for a little treat along the way. Of course, that routine was about to be challenged—in that there were no blanket and no doors on the kayak. Of course, not being well-versed on the natural transitions for canine water training did not matter much to me; after all, how hard could it be for a natural-born swimmer? I could see it clearly: water, dog paddle, and days of swimming fun ahead.

As we paddled, the whimpering continued but changed in tone. Was that the whimpering of a dog hearing the call of his ancestors to embrace the water? Or perhaps the siren song calling a delusional sailor to the impending depths?

After some time paddling and periods of verbal encouragement for Toby to embrace his genetic call-ing, it was increasingly evident that a subtle nudge was warranted. However, the nudge was more like the stiff arm of an elite running back headed for the goal line. The only problem was that Toby wasn't carrying a ball, there wasn't a goal line, and he didn't land on a hard surface. Captured in millisecond snapshots, Toby went from being airborne to being absent. There was no stride, no approach, no leap—only a push. And the entry appeared to have no exit.

The canine Michael Phelps sank like a rock—as did my heart. Whether instinctively or hoping that Toby would do the same, I held my breath. Concurrently, my wife began yelling hysterically at me for my foolish act that was going to take the life of our beloved Toby. After the eternity of several seconds, a paw emerged, followed by another. With the genetically proven webbed pads engaged, creating enough lift for the svelte canine, Toby overcame the idiocy of his owner's delusional dreams and found his inner Lab. However, rather than paddle alongside the kayak, a vehicle of torture as he now likely saw it, he navigated toward the first sight of land.

He zigged. We zagged. With dogged determination he created the separation dreamed of by elite triathletes during an open-water swim. Frantically, we paddled to catch this prodigy forced into service before the adrenaline of the moment abated. Fortunately, our powerful strokes were enough to close the gap of our webbed-footed canine. Cautiously coming alongside without submerging Toby, we grasped his collar and hoisted him from his aquatic training grounds. I am not certain who was breathing harder, Toby or I, but for a moment, there was a tremendous sigh of relief—perhaps for us all.

None too impressed by the event and having the natural response to an extended, unanticipated cold exposure, Toby looked at me for a moment, then turned his head toward the shoreline and released his bladder on top of the kayak.

This was not quite the indoctrination to early canine water-sport training that I had anticipated and perhaps the causative reason he became a shoreline wanderer

in the future. Shortly thereafter we all found solace in the ability to stand on dry land as we stepped from the kayak. As Toby shook off the remaining water from his coat, he regained his energetic puppy demeanor and began playfully jumping and prancing about the shore. His movements fell short of Swan Lake, but the choreographed silent dance was inspiring—although not the same without a tutu.

As we packed up the kayak for the day and loaded into the truck, Toby leapt onto the back seat. Within moments he had found the canine version of a charging pad and was out. His only apparent movements on the way home appeared to be a series of graceful, intermittent strokes of his legs in full paddle.

CHAPTER 6:

Frivolity in the Snow

THERE ARE ALWAYS FIRSTS IN LIFE. AND IN THE early stages of life, that is more commonly true for all of us. For Toby that was no different. And despite having an unwavering daily canine routine with the predictable pleasures of food, play, and poo, we tried to vary experiences for Toby—or perhaps for ourselves—as much as possible. I am not certain if it was his fault, ours, or the beautiful synergy that began with his arrival, but there was just something about new experiences. Maybe Darius Rucker, a modern-day country musician, heard about Toby's desire for the unknown when he penned the lyric, "When was the last time you did something for the first time?" Perhaps not, but it certainly applied to our masked bandit throughout every stage of life.

For the longest time we thought Toby had some genetic challenges. Not because of his appearance or an off-putting temperament. Not that he had additional or dysmorphic appendages. However, although Toby's physique and disposition certainly took after the Labrador genetics he received from his mother, it appeared that he also received a double dose of the genetic code for puppy zoomies—and only half the amount of DNA programming for a timely developmental transition to adulthood. Yes, Toby was a late bloomer. Quite frankly he thought he was a puppy until he reached double digits—far closer to the day he would receive his AARP card for many years of good barking.

Much like John Muir and the wilderness-minded people of today, our family loves to embrace the outdoors. And although we never heard the auditory call of the mountains, we fully embraced that "in every walk with nature, one receives far more than [one] seeks"—and so did Toby. It wasn't the particular activity, such as hiking, biking, paddling, or sitting, but being together in the presence of nature that seemed to call us. And we would respond with Toby in tow.

As any good Carolinians, we love snow. It does not come often enough and never sticks around for long—but when it does, it is absolutely incredible. The Piedmont, with its rolling hills, deciduous trees, and farmland stretching to the Blue Ridge, is a winter wonderland when blanketed in snow. However, unlike those predictable climates where meteorologists can forecast not only that snow will be coming but that it will remain for the next six months, our region apparently poses some predictability challenges. However, one thing often holds true: add a little elevation to the mix, and you might just find what it is you are looking for.

With great anticipation we awoke to gray skies and, despite the previous night's forecast, no evidence of snow. Rather than a sugar plum fairy performing to Carolina Mountain music, we dreamed of our beloved Toby frolicking around in the new-fallen snow. However, the dream-driven excitement of snow-filled frivolity departed quickly as Toby's routine morning walk was met by rain and sleet. Wet dog. Shattered plans.

After a good toweling off due to my wife's olfactory hypersensitivity to the unique smell of wet dog, Toby no longer looked like a drowned rat, and after a few spritzes of his canine cologne, he was "The Man" once again. However, after one look at the pile of snow gear and the outdoor thermometer perched well above freezing, we had an idea, and Toby sensed it as we started packing up. The mountains were calling, and we had to go.

With the blissfully restored enthusiasm of a child celebrating their first birthday—yes, the one with cake and frosting smeared all over their face—we loaded up into our well-worn Toyota Tacoma in pursuit of that frozen spectacle. As we headed westward toward the Blue Ridge Parkway, the drone of the tires on the highway provided the backdrop for conversation balanced with the usual rubbing of Toby's velvety soft ears and his incessant panting from excitement. Toby *loved* "going for a ride." Whether he was a canine descendant of the Roman Empire or not, there was just something innate for him about riding in his "chariot." The distance did not matter—it was in the journey that he found great joy. Something that perhaps took me a little too long to understand.

The gray skies darkened as we began the climb into the mountains, and with it, the sleet began to lighten and give way to the glorious appearance of falling snow. The wet ground became blanketed in white as the elevation increased and the temperature dropped. Our excitement was sensed by Toby and reflected as full-body wiggles of overwhelming joy.

Turning off the highway and onto the Blue Ridge Parkway, we soon found what we had dreamed about: an expansive white playground. The drone of the tires was replaced with the crunching sound of compacting snow. Everything else fell silent from the ongoing blanketing of snow. Of course, it was hard to tell who was more excited about the opportunity: me or Toby. As we bundled up to head out into the snowstorm, the climb of anticipation up the foothills proved to be an overwhelming success…snow, snow, and more snow.

As Toby jumped from the truck and his paws hit the snow for the first time, he froze—figuratively. He looked around at the endless array of falling snowflakes, likely sensing the auditory dampening that came with

them. For a moment, he just stood there embracing the pure bliss of heavenly fluff that continued to fall without request or denial.

Then he embraced his inner reindeer and began jumping and prancing through the snow. Fortunately, his long tether allowed for an unfettered exploration of the glorious, icy goodness. At times it appeared as if Toby had created his own winter "mud run" as he was conquering obstacles fictitiously created in the fallen snow. Between these demonstrations of cardiovascular and physical strength, we played fetch and catch with well-packed snowballs rather than the usual tennis ball or KONG. As each ball was tossed, Toby would launch into the air to prevent anyone from intercepting this prized possession—only to immediately destroy the snowball in the awaiting playful jaws of a dog that loved eating ice. Full of life, he sat there with snow all about his muzzle looking like a bearded dragon—or perhaps the Carolinian version of a canine Yeti. Pure. Joy.

As we loaded up into the truck, exhilaratingly tired and just a bit cold, without any evidence of impending frost bite, I glanced into the back seat. There was Toby, sitting on his blanket with his paws on the edge of the window, looking at the snow with his tail still wagging—silently, I could hear him begging, *please*, just one more time. That wouldn't be our last snow adventure, but it was certainly our first. It's a simple reminder that in all the paths you take in life, make certain a few of them are in the snow.

CHAPTER 7:

Houdini in the Ruff

MORE THAN A CENTURY BEFORE THE BIRTH OF Toby, Harry Houdini, a magician noted for his sensational escape feats, was born. And while I cannot find evidence that Houdini trained canines in the art of escape, it appears as though some distant ancestors of our canine companion must have seen a demonstration or two. For each of us, there comes a time in life when we are awakened to our calling. For Toby it was embracing this unique yet previously unknown talent: the unfathomable, magical escape.

Now while Toby had never spent time watching the likes of David Copperfield, apparently, he must have come from a long line of magician canines. Afterall, his mother was able to make an entire litter of nine puppies disappear from the Humane Society quite quickly.

We are quite certain it was a staged event. Planned over months of mental gymnastics and careful consideration. We always knew Toby had a keen eye, but we never thought he was paying close attention to his crate. Now I certainly don't blame him for taking up his magic routine. After all, how much fun can you have inside your kennel—with such miserable luxuries as the soft plushness of your toy critters, the finest bedding that Kirkland Signature has to offer, water, and a KONG laden with crunchy peanut butter—when the rest of the world is waiting to be explored? Well at least waiting once finished with the peanut butter.

Routines can be good—whether for the dog or the dog's person. However sometimes even the smallest shift out of a routine can trigger a landslide of questions. Perhaps it should come as no surprise given the adventures to date, but after returning from work and walking up the stairs to set Toby free, there he was, sitting at the door waiting for the return of his family. Tail thumping. Bright eyed. And overjoyed that playtime was about to start.

But it was in that moment that a perplexing thought crossed my mind. That moment when the synaptic brain processes aren't quite aligned. When not everything seems to be computing. Wasn't Toby locked in his kennel this morning? Even more concerning was the potential bowel-related surprises that might be awaiting underfoot although so far undetected by scent. Speaking of bowel or bladder missteps, have you ever noticed that such accidents usually happen to be only inches away from an area that would be far less absorbent and much easier to clean?

As my "favorite-person-in-the-world-status" welcome home greeting associated with intermittent barking and incessant tail wagging continued, I paused just for a moment and was reminded that contentment in life can be a fairly simple thing. Even a genuinely warm greeting from a loyal four-legged companion. Peace. Love. Joy. Such a demonstration of unwavering attention and unconditional dedication reminded me of a quote that said, "I would love to be the man my dog thinks I am." So true.

After failing to find any puppy toilet surprises on the floor, we walked over to his daily resting location. There in its designated location was his crate. However, the otherwise large cuboid structure was oddly flat, with its weight compressing the life out of those chew toys. I starred at the kennel—perplexed at what I was seeing before me—and then turned back to Toby. He sat there. Tail thumping, bright eyed, and ready to go play. I have no doubt that he was replaying the events around his incredible escape routine in his mind. I have heard of sporting dogs trained for hunting, tracking, retrieving and obstacles—but never had I heard of Houdini crate-escape training.

I stood there with possible permutations of his escape running through my mind—and although I know he couldn't read my mind, I know he wished

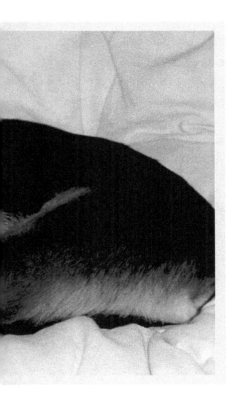

the converse were true. After shaking my head a few more times, I opened his crate and locked it back into place, setting free his collection of chew toys that appeared uninjured after the collapse.

Over the next few weeks, Houdini would return. Despite all the kennel training books we could find and the addition of zip ties at critical locations about his crate, Toby would surprise us again and again on our return home. Tail thumping, bright eyed. No scratches, no scars—no signs of trauma. Given that we didn't find escapism under the troubleshooting sections of any crate training guides, it seemed that this was quite the anomaly.

Whether a young Jedi-in-training or excelling in teleportation, Toby had a gift. Perhaps it was that he was much happier exploring the world outside the confines of his crate. I suspect that truth would resonate with each one of us as well.

From that day forward, the crate was retired. Aside from learning how to open levered doors and navigate cabinet pulls, Houdini kept a low profile. Maybe he wasn't faced with expanding his performance repertoire or didn't feel the need to demonstrate his craft, but we knew as the years went on that one day soon, like each one of us, he would perform his final disappearing act.

CHAPTER 8:

Backcountry Adventures

I CANNOT IMAGINE THERE ARE MANY DOGS THAT FAN-tasize about navigating the backcountry wilderness with a weighted pack on their backs. And while I have never taken a mule ride to the bottom of the Grand Canyon, I have carried my fair share of packs along incredible stretches of national parks. There is something to be said about carrying your own essentials for survival amid the incredible wilderness around you. And the simple state of calming exuberance that comes when you can finally unload your pack, set up camp, and relax in awe of what surrounds you. In addition to breathing in the incredible environment, have you ever noticed

how much better food tastes after a long day of hiking or around an open fire? It didn't take Toby long to figure that out either—especially after having received his own canine saddle bags while still young.

Having grown up a stone's throw from Mount Rainier in the state of Washington, escaping on trails in the Cascades may have been common, but it is truly miraculous. From Longmire to Paradise, hiking amid century-old evergreens up to rock-covered vistas just to catch a glimpse of the sleeping giant was breathtaking. Now living near the Appalachian Mountains of North Carolina, it is a different type of beauty. It is the ruggedness despite the limited elevation that makes this ancient backcountry unique. One of our favorite locations is the Linville Gorge Wilderness Area, just off the Blue Ridge Parkway.

As mentioned previously, the chance to go for a ride in the truck was something Toby embraced fully. It brought freedom and adventure in abundance. Although preceding this adventure, he knew there was something different. Perhaps it was the weeklong preparation that started with his daily exercise, now including his hiking saddle bags. Or perhaps it was the slight increase in duration of walking concurrent with the ever-increasing pack weight. Regardless, he may not have known exactly what was coming, but he knew it was something exciting.

Of course, with Toby and his endless motivation for food, providing a special treat after donning his pack went a long way toward encouraging our preparation. In addition, the fact that his pack was filled with bags of dog food and treats for his pack training certainly helped. That lingering scent of gustatory abundance was more than enough encouragement for this pooch. Just saying the magic words, "Hey Toby, let's get your pack" would send him into a Pavlovian frenzy. With the door opened, he would fly down the stairs to the garage with barely a paw touching the stairs, slinging drool side to side. For Toby, just the anticipation was pure joy.

When the day came for our backcountry adventure, Toby and his saddle bags joined a ragamuffin band of outdoor enthusiasts. Of course, not aware of pack mule etiquette, our almost alpha-male Toby failed to recognize that his enthusiasm to be out front would intermittently take out any would-be hikers with the canine karate saddle-bag knee drop. For those having experienced it before, it is commonly followed by an orthopedic referral. Being tethered to Toby and his knock-down packs presented no lack of initial challenges. However, with a little extra distance between us and the others, heightened attention to foot positioning on the more treacherous section, and a few extra treats of encouragement, we found a balance successfully navigating the trails despite the myriad new sounds and smells.

Whether navigating over (or under) downed trees, slipping over damp fallen leaves, or stepping down the intermittent rock faces littering the trail, with each step Toby embraced something new. New sounds were also abundant. The crashing of rocks released from the peaks due to years of erosion across the gorge. The crash, crash, thump of limbs falling from dying Eastern hemlocks. And at times he would hear or find a scent of a nearby deer and become overwhelmed by the inherited trait to point. Good dog.

As we dropped down Babel Tower toward the Linville River, the silence was palpable. Aside from the ticktock of Toby's pack moving side to side, there was only the sound of the water rushing through the ancient gorge. Although, I thought I could hear the faint sound of banjos and mountain music in the distance. Peaceful. Breathtaking. There was something magical about descending one of the oldest gorges in North America with our pack-laden pooch.

At one junction during our expedition, we were separated from the pack. Following the lead of the few with us, we were hiking up a narrow, dirt-packed path through a hillside dense with mountain laurels and foliage. Without warning Toby began to yelp. Within seconds I felt the sting that likely triggered his response. A ground nest of yellow jackets erupted underfoot, and we were amid the maelstrom. Without thought Toby and I bounded into the thicket and looked like two whitetails leaping bush over bush for safety. Minutes later the assault ended. Standing high above the ambush, we assessed the damage. Toby's mouth, face and ears were a bit swollen—but not so much as to impact

his ability to scarf down a treat and a little water.

Along this adventure, we also experienced some additional surprises and created a few new words related to them. Hammock-diver. S'mores face. Bear-dung breath. Tent digger. You can only imagine the stories that go along with each—and the images in your head alone certainly cannot do them justice.

To exit the gorge, you must navigate a granite wall on the river's edge. Bouldering along the river can pose a few challenges. The damp surfaces are like hiking on angled sheets of ice. The pitches rise and fall with the only reprieve being a quick dip into the cooling waters of the river. It's one thing to navigate this with a trekking pole and your pack; it is quite another when you have a fifty-pound canine depending on you to make the right move.

Fortunately, Toby could see the movement of the other team members in front of us. Of course, replicating that approach was a bit more of a challenge. Anticipating Toby's movement and balancing it with each step was difficult yet redundant. Trekking pole in the left hand sounding the water depth, check. Right hand grasping Toby's saddlebag handle, lifting him across the next pitch, check. Both legs anchored on the slick boulders, check. Repeat. With Toby's intermittent whimpering, whether due to the excitement or concern, I felt my heart rate rise as we navigated the rock wall. Being able to see the path as demonstrated by the person in front of you is one thing—trying to replicate it with a dog in hand, let alone trying to verbalize the plan to Toby, was something quite different.

After bouldering down to the river's edge, the final stretch required lifting Toby across a ten-foot chasm between rock edges while stepping waist deep into the water and attempting to find several stable footholds. Chosen wisely, you avoid a full-body immersion. One misstep and you enjoy a refreshing, cold spa experience. Fortunately for Toby those on the other side of the chasm were able to grab and hoist him safely on the first attempt. Good dog, Toby. Although we escaped relatively unscathed, the whimpers and tail-wagging tornado remain imprinted in my mind, with still images of each step along the way.

Over the years to come, Toby would find this recurrent adventure revitalizing. Whether it was the opportunity to break out of his daily routine and take in the abundance of sights, sounds, smells, and foods or just enjoy some dedicated time with a ragamuffin band of adventure-seekers wasn't so clear. What was clear was that he embraced the opportunity as much as, if not more than, anyone else. Even if it meant being precariously placed along the river's edge.

CHAPTER 9:

Surfing without the Waves

TOBY HAD A PREDILECTION FOR ALL SORTS OF trouble. This became increasingly clear as he entered the later prime of his life. While that did not take the form of seeking out critters that would leave an indelible mark on him (or our back porch), it did mean searching for new "opportunities" whenever and wherever his snout would lead.

For him the kitchen was sacred ground. From it permeated a vast cornucopia of smells. Some sweet, others savory, some pungent, others unforgettable. Not only did the kitchen hold an endless array of olfactory delights; it also held the trough in which

Toby's daily feedings would occur. Apparently trained by Pavlov himself, when that time of day or the sound of the kibble container would shake, Toby would materialize faster than his favorite pooch superhero, Bolt. At attention? Absolutely. And drooling like a thickened, midspring runoff waterfall. Rather than eating patiently and enjoying every morsel, Toby took a page from the book of his youth when competing with eight other siblings for sustenance from his mother. If food inhalation was a canine competition category, Toby would be an elite athlete.

Over time, he became a bit more opportunistic. Perhaps it was the growth from puppyhood to adolescence to middle age fostered by the tasty morsels that occasionally fell from our kids as they navigated life between highchairs and utensils. If Toby's increasing girth had anything to do with our kids' hand-eye coordination with eating, they failed miserably. I am quite certain that life must have appeared like an episode out of *Cloudy with a Chance of Meatballs* as foods of all shapes and sizes would fall from the sky.

The upside was that the floor was relatively devoid of food debris aside from the occasional piece of lettuce or onion. The downside was that dog slobber could make even the nicest of hardwood floors become a virtual skating rink for those unaware. Never experienced it? Give it a try.

So as the holidays approached, we started the annual routine of planning the festive meals and adding items to the pantry and the fridge. This particular year we were planning to dabble in the culinary pursuit of the best roast beef ever. Perfectly selected with a recipe that would make the faint of heart succumb to the forces of gravity while others have a salivary storm in anticipation of the first bite. And in a moment that seems to live on in infamy in our family, the roast was left on the counter while we attended to errands outside of the house.

On returning home all seemed well—except the usual blissful greeting wasn't present, only Toby sitting sheepishly in the corner. There wasn't anything in the kitchen to trigger a memory of my preparatory failure—no pan on the ground, no mess to be cleaned. Nothing. It was only when my beloved wife started to inquire about the roast that the story began to unfold. Of course, the fact that Toby appeared to be in his third trimester despite being a neutered male dog helped. And that his breath smelled identical to the well-seasoned roast helped close the case. So that year we settled for grilled cheese—well, not really.

In the years that followed, it was impossible to erase that incredible gastrological delight for Toby. If there was even the slightest scent of something tantalizing anywhere in the kitchen, he would wait for the moment to explore. The latch of the basement door closing would signal the opportunity, like an undefeated fighter entering the ring. Toby would jab left and right with his paw, sight unseen, with the hopes of landing a few good blows onto an unexpecting dish or container.

When caught in the act, he would simply retreat to the floor with a slight cowering of shame as he awaited the oncoming inquisition—only to tempt fate the next time the opportunity would present itself.

I suspect that for any carnivorous creature, once you've experienced the palatal pleasure of USDA Grade A beef, it's hard to go back. For Toby, no greater truth could be said. I've heard it said that some people are born to ride the waves. Toby, well, he surfs counters. Roast beef will do that to you.

CHAPTER 10:

Taking Out the Trash

ACH OF US HAVE THEM. IT MAY BE A WEEKLY ENdeavor, for others, perhaps daily. You know what they are: chores. Those things in life that we must do to keep things neat and tidy. For some it may be the act of making your bed first thing in the morning to trigger your resolve for the day ahead (thanks, General McCrystal). For others it may be attending to the plants or cleaning a particular area of the house. Toby's favorite chore was most certainly taking out the trash.

Early in his life, we attempted to train him to bring in the newspaper and even try to carry a cold beverage from the refrigerator to a parched recipient in another room. Abstract failures. Not due to a lack of Toby's intellect, but likely due to my lack of canine training

prowess. The attempts with the newspapers led to the shredding of the entire paper, except for the occasional comic section or grocery ads. I didn't consider that a coincidence. The beverages would arrive on occasion, but the combination of dog slobber on the outside of the can and the carbonated explosion on opening led to the cancellation of that training regimen.

While Toby ensured that the floor around the table was particularly clear of any food items, he seemed perplexed regarding our post meal routine. At the end of every meal, despite evident puppy-eyed protests from Toby, every remaining tasty morsel from the dinner plate that could not be saved for heavenly leftovers would be scraped into an unknown void hidden behind a wall of plastic.

And he saw that routine repeated daily. Open door, pull slider—goodbye, mealtime treasures. After Toby saw this process repeated thousands of times over more than ten years, it became hardwired. Have you ever been amazed at some of the things you learn just by watching?

For Toby those olfactory receptors that are ten thousand times stronger than our sense of smell would be the source of this daily temptation. Over time the vison of reaching that receptacle, the holy grail of smells, became too much for him. And while we had gone through episodes of child-proofing our house with variable success, we thought our dog-proofing days were behind us.

However, at one point, the Houdini mindset returned to Toby with a twist. Instead of setting himself free, why not free those tempting morsels that are trapped behind a door and inside a container? Open door, pull slider…

I've never dealt with the destruction of a tornado, but coming home to coffee grounds, orange peels, eggshells, and the past four days' food debris scattered about the kitchen floor is far from exhilarating. The fact that the back door wasn't open and that we don't routinely see racoons in our yard led to only one possible culprit: our masked bandit. Where was Toby during the investigation? Hiding

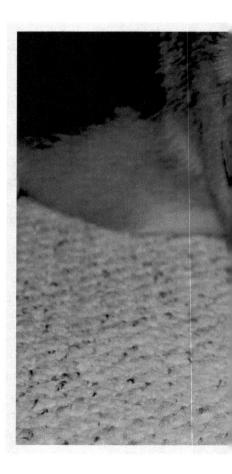

in the corner of the room. And while we were not able to confirm it at the time, his bowel habits over the coming days led to his conviction—guilty as charged.

I'm not certain we were ever able to fully prevent Toby from getting into the cabinets until age took away most of his frontal incisors. Every child-proof lock he removed. Every tension band he would chew off. Zip ties, ha. The only way to prevent another refuse explosion was to either put the trash bag in the sink or bring Toby along in the car. Perhaps that was what he wanted all along.

CHAPTER 11:

Life's Curtain Call

WHAT IS THE MEASURE OF A LIFE LIVED WELL? Is it a duration of time, the events during that time span, the relationships formed, or perhaps the depth of relationships established? For Toby it was perhaps all the above. For nearly fifteen years, he was part of the family. A loyal companion like no other. The "first-born" into our marriage with an uncharacteristic endless love for his owners despite their downfalls as parents. And that desirable canine presence that was loved by all who came to know him. During his fourteenth year, age-associated challenges began to show their predictable presence. No longer was the daily walk filled with frolic and playfulness, but often the reminder that total joint surgery was designed for a reason.

But he never really grew into the frail elder states-
man of dogs even much younger than him. While he
no longer flexed the glamour muscles of his youth,
only slightly was his skeleton more visible beneath
the increasingly graying black-and-tan coat. Although
increasingly his time spent dreaming of his past (mis)
adventures surpassed that of the active times where he
was alert, attentive, and available.

Timing is everything…but never easy. The day after
Christmas began like any post-holiday morning, full
of joy from the previous day, gratitude for the eternal
celebration, and great anticipation for the inevitable
cleanup that would follow. However, after we woke
and gave Toby his good-morning pat on the head, he
staggered to his feet with an uneasiness and instability
that was not present the day before. Watching him get
to his feet, it was evident that something wasn't right.
As he walked to the kitchen, his gait was unsteady,
with intermittent listing to the right and left. Yet there
wasn't a stroke code response team or the benefit of
calling 911 despite precisely knowing the time when
Toby was last known normal.

After navigating his morning walk, which now
was much more of a stagger to the receptacle of daily sustenance, his food bowl, he looked up with eyes
of anticipation for the glorious nuggets of goodness
that had defined his breakfast for many years. However
today the premeal drooling that was commonly triggered by the sound of food hitting the bowl was much

worse. And despite the ability to get the morsels into his mouth, the ability to swallow had now turned into a failed spin cycle that was no longer coordinated and led to intermittent episodes of coughing and gagging.

I've spent time around people during those acute stroke episodes and those whose bodies were failing, trapped in the grasp of what is inevitable for each of us. It isn't easy to accept but even more difficult to embrace. To find the balance of doing what is right and doing the right thing. But the beauty of the moment was that the events of that day didn't define Toby but started to trigger the events that he may not recall, but that we would never forget. And perhaps it was not necessarily the event itself that conjured such a range of emotional and neurosynaptic responses, but the realization of humanity reflected through the life of a dog.

I always believed Toby was most happy when he was able to run free in the rolling hills of the countryside. Where he was able to breathe the air only tainted by the scent of wild turkey, deer, and those pesky rabid squirrels. Where the trails held the truth of those that had been most recently present and the footprints confirmed what his nose already knew. But perhaps it was I who was most happy there also. And the beauty of that space was only amplified by the fact that it came amid the silence.

And silence filled much of the coming days. It wasn't due to a cancel-cultural influence related to his ailing health—after all, dogs don't talk, not in the manner we

think anyway, and certainly Toby was not one to complain unless you kidnapped his priceless bowl of kibble. However, his ability to navigate his ADLs, those activities of daily living, had changed substantially. No longer did the sound of food hitting his bowl bring about the Pavlovian responses of his youth but rather the struggle to maintain homeostasis. No longer was the walk to the backyard a pleasurable reprieve of sights, sounds, and smells—but now the challenge of navigating steps and tremoring legs that moved erratically without coordinated purpose and released different chemicals in his brain that no longer brought joy. Even after I would gently carry him down the steps and steady him as he sniffed the ground, he would look up with his deep-penetrating, well-aged eyes just for assurance of my presence. As things progressed he even required a boost in the rear just to relieve himself with dignity.

How I longed for a return to his frisbee-fetching canine craziness, but it was not to be. Reminiscing consumed the abundance of moments. These moments were almost overwhelming as I could hear the sweet sound of his enthusiastic bark beginning to fade into the distance. Yet despite his slower tempo of life, the glorious dance of abundant adventures was reflected in his tired eyes.

His final last few weeks were spent intermittently camouflaged on a soft fleece blanket mirroring the softened brown of his graying coat and accompanied by his feline sister. It was one of those fake sheepskin fleece blankets that held warmth—and odors. And Toby loved it. And while not able to position his body in the same merry-go-round of life as he could in his youth, the sigh of relief when he would collapse on it almost echoed the words written across the blanket— Good Dog.

I have heard it said that how you treat your dog in its final days reflects how you will treat others in your family when the time comes. Perhaps it reflects how you hope others will care for you. I hope that both are correct. There is a true communion in the relationship with our dogs that we hope to have with other people.

Sometimes it holds water, other times not so. Where else can we find a level of companionship that fully embraces the ultimate description of love—endlessly patient, eternally kind, unconditional, unwavering, and fully devoted without criticism? At times I know my wife and kids would welcome me to be the man that Toby thinks I am—and while I ascribe to be just that, I often fail in the attempt. Unconditional indeed.

CHAPTER 12:

The Last Adventure

TOBY WAS ALWAYS FOND OF GOING TO THE VETER-
inarian. Perhaps it was just the opportunity to
saddle up in the back seat of the truck and lum-
ber down the road like the Lone Ranger and Tonto in
search of adventure. Or the abundance of incredible
smells left from the previous visitors on the approach
into the office—canines, felines, and humans alike.
However, as I loaded him into my truck for one last
ride, the emotions of a life well lived overwhelmed my
spirit once again. Selfishly I struggled to move from the
sense of impending loss as I wiped cascading tears from
my face to the celebration of joy for the adventures
shared and the life lived together.

It was time, and he knew it. For the past several
weeks, we embraced the life of our Good Dog through

the lens of his life while perhaps not recognizing the dimming fire behind his own near-blind eyes. Maybe it was the hope that the neurosynaptic fibers damaged from the stroke that he recently suffered would miraculously heal themselves, and he would regain function. Perhaps it was that we could still see the life in him, just now subdued from age and time of a life lived well. Selfishly, I knew it was due to the difficult challenge we all face in life—knowing when to let go and recognizing that keeping him alive wasn't what was right for him but was good for us.

Reaching into the back seat, I rubbed those velvety ears now well grayed like the rest of his face and passed him a morsel of goodness…just because. Then we slowly rolled down the driveway for our last time—our last adventure together.

As the drone of the tires on the road calmed my emotional peaks and valleys, I pressed rewind on that VHS tape in my mind, stopping fifteen years earlier. The replay brought the corners of my mouth just a little bit higher while opening the floodgate of my lachrymal apparatus. I began to reminisce about the endless memories of the preceding years together. Each smile followed by a chuckle and paired with a tear. Each chuckle matched by a little shaking of the head, a muttering of good grief, and followed closely by a heavy sigh.

Good dog…those were the last words that I said to him as I embraced him in the veterinarian's office as his breathing ceased. A moment in time that still brings tears as an aging memory replays the event. But the beauty of a life lived well is simple. His stories are my stories—are my family's stories. Not to be quickly forgotten but cherished and perhaps embellished as time moves forward. Whether you are caught standing naked in the rain or flummoxed by yet another Houdini routine, everyone should be so blessed to have their lives touched by someone like Toby.

One thing that remains is that Good Dog blanket—or at least part of it—and the essence of Toby in those final weeks. Thanks to my lovely wife's creativity, each member of our family has this little gift tucked away in a special place, like the priceless treasure that it is. And on those days where your tank is just a little bit empty, the kindness of the world didn't quite measure up, or you need the corners of your mouth to turn up just a little bit more, a gentle rub of that blanket warms the soul like few other things. Memories? Cherished. Forgotten? Never.